To Parents and Teachers:

We hope you and the children will enjoy reading this story in English and French. It is simply told, but not *simplified,* so that both versions are quite natural. However, there is lots of repetition for practicing pronunciation, for helping develop memory skills, and for reinforcing comprehension.

At the back of the book, there is a simple picture dictionary with key words as well as a basic pronunciation guide to the whole story.

Here are a few suggestions on using the book:

- First, read the story aloud in English to become familiar with it. Treat it like any other picture book. Look at the drawings, talk about the story, the characters, and so on.

- Then look at the picture dictionary and repeat the key words in French. Make this an active exercise. Ask the children to say the words out loud instead of reading them.

- Go back and read the story again, this time in English and French. Don't worry if your pronunciation isn't quite correct. Just have fun trying it out. If necessary, check the guide at the back of the book, but you'll soon pick up how to say the French words.

- When you think you and the children are ready, try reading the story in French. Ask the children to say it with you. Only ask them to read it if they seem eager to try. The spelling could be confusing and discourage them.

- Above all, encourage the children, and give them lots of praise. They are usually quite unselfconscious, so let them be children and play act, try out different voices, and have fun. This is an excellent way to build confidence for acquiring foreign language skills.

First edition for the United States and Canada published 1996 by Barron's Educational Series, Inc.
Text © Copyright 1996 by b small publishing, Surrey, England
Illustrations © Copyright 1996 by Lucy Keijser

Address all inquiries to: Barron's Educational Series, Inc., 250 Wireless Boulevard, Hauppauge, New York 11788
International Standard Book Number 0-8120-6581-6   Library of Congress Catalog Card Number 95-53762
Printed in Hong Kong   6789   9598   98765432

Happy birthday!

Bon anniversaire!

Mary Risk
Pictures by Lucy Keijser
French by Jacqueline Jansen

BARRON'S

It's my birthday.

C'est mon anniversaire.

Here are all my friends.
Hi! Hello! Come in, everyone!

Voilà tous mes amis.
Salut! Bonjour! Entrez tous!

All these presents for me?
What an amazing mask!

Tous ces cadeaux pour moi?
Quel masque génial!

And I love this dinosaur!

Et j'adore ce dinosaure!

Let's blow some bubbles.
They're huge.

Faisons des bulles de savon!
Elles sont énormes, non?

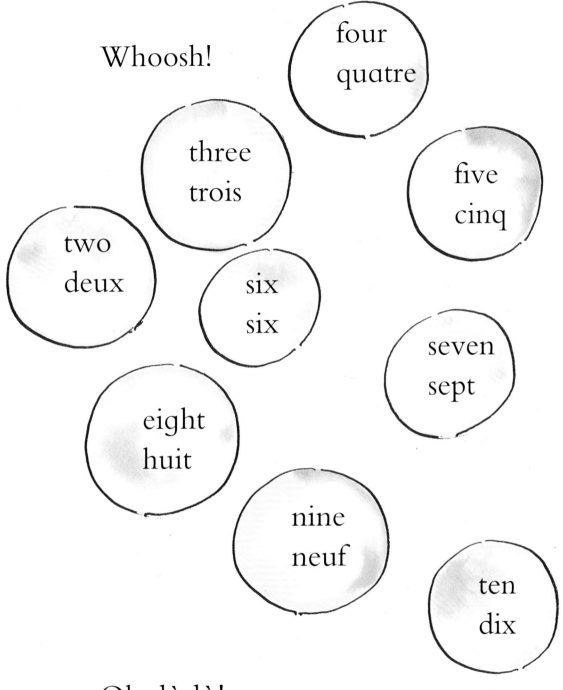

Where have they all gone?

Où sont-elles passées?

Oh! Look at Sarah!

Eh! Regardez Sarah!

Balloons!
Can I have one?

Des ballons!
Est ce que je peux en avoir un?

The red one's for you.
Le rouge est pour toi.

The green one's for me.
Le vert est pour moi.

The blue one's for Peter.
Le bleu est pour Pierre.

The purple one's for Clare.
Le violet est pour Claire.

This is fantastic!
This is fun!

Ça c'est super!
Ça c'est marrant!

Oh dear! Good-bye, balloons!

Oh mon dieu! Au revoir, les ballons!

Have you lost your balloon?
Never mind, don't cry!

Tu as perdu ton ballon?
Ce n'est pas grave! Ne pleure pas!

Are you hungry?
Have some cake.

Vous avez faim? Prenez du gâteau.

Are you thirsty?
Have a drink.

Tu as soif? Sers-toi à boire.

That was a great party.
Thank you for having us.

C'était une chouette fête.
Merci pour l'invitation.

Look! The balloons!

Regardez! Les ballons!

Good-bye!

Au revoir!

Pronouncing French

Don't worry if your pronunciation isn't quite correct. The important thing is to be willing to try. The pronunciation guide here will help but it cannot be completely accurate:

• Read the guide as naturally as possible, as if it were English.

• When reading, stress the letters in *italics* (e.g., bohn *zhoor*).

• Generally final consonants in French are silent (salut/sah *luh*).

If you can, ask a French speaking person to help and move on as soon as possible to speaking the words without the guide.

Note: French adjectives usually have two forms, one for masculine and one for feminine nouns. They often look very similar but are pronounced slightly differently, e.g., **vert** and **verte** (see the word list below).

Words Les Mots
leh moh

happy birthday!
bon anniversaire

bohn ah nee vehr *sahr*

cake
le gâteau

luh gah *toh*

present
le cadeau

luh kah *doh*

balloon
le ballon
luh bah *loh*

**soap
bubble**
la bulle de savon
lah buhl deh sah *voh*

mask
le masque
luh mahsk

hi
salut
sah *luh*

hello
bonjour
bohn *zhoor*

dinosaur
le dinosaure
luh dee noh *zohr*

thank you
merci
mehr *see*

good-bye
au revoir
oh ru *vwah*

friend
l'ami, l'amie
lahmee, lahmee

great
chouette
shwhet

amazing
génial
zheh nee*ahl*

fantastic
super
suh *pehr*

fun
marrant
mah *roh*

party
la fête
lah fett

red
rouge
roosh

purple
violet/violette
vioh *leh*/vioh *leht*

blue
bleu/bleue
bluh/bluh

green
vert/verte
vehr/vehrt

A simple guide to pronouncing this French story

C'est mon anniversaire.
seh mohn ah nee vehr *sahr*

Voilà tous mes amis.
vwah *lah* toohs mehs amee

Salut! Bonjour! Entrez tous!
sah *luh* bon *zhoor* ehn *treh* toos

Tous ces cadeaux pour moi?
too say cah *doh* poor mwah

Quel masque génial!
kehl mahsk zheh *neeahl*

Et j'adore ce dinosaure!
eh jah *dohr* ceh dee noh *zohr*

Faisons des bulles de savon.
feh *soh* deh buhl de sah *voh*

Elles sont énormes, non?
ehl sohn eh *norh* nohn

un, deux, trois, quatre, cinq, six, sept, huit, neuf, dix
ewn, duh, twah, *kah* truh, sahnk, seess, seht, wheet, nuhf, deess

Oh! la! la!
o lah lah

Où sont-elles passées?
oo sohnt ehl pah *say*

Eh! Regardez Sarah!
eh ruh gahr *day* Sah *rah*

Des ballons!
deh bal *loh*

Est-ce que je peux en avoir un?
ehss kuh zhuh pooh ahn ah *vwahr* uhn

Le rouge est pour toi.
luh woosh eh poor twah

Le vert est pour moi.
luh vehr eh poor mwah

Le bleu est pour Pierre.
luh blooh eh poor pee *ehr*

Le violet est pour Claire.
luh vioh *leh* eh poor clahr

Ça c'est super!
sah seh suh *pehr*

C'est marrant!
sah seh mah *roh*

Oh mon dieu!
oh mohn deeuh

Au revoir, les ballons!
oh ru *vwah* leh bahl *loh*

Tu as perdu ton ballon?
tew ah pehr *duh* tohn bah *loh*

Ce n'est pas grave! Ne pleure pas!
suh neh pah grahv, nuh ploohr pah

Avez-vous faim?
ah *vay* voo fan

Prenez du gâteau.
prah *neh* duh gah toh

Tu as soif?
too ah swahf

Sers-toi à boire.
sehr twah ah bwahr

C'était une chouette fête.
seh teh ewn shwhet feht

Merci pour l'invitation.
mair *see* poor lan veet assee *ohn*

Regardez! Les ballons!
ruh gahr *day* leh bahl *loh*

Au revoir!
oh ru *vwah*